Sweet Pea

The Homeless Dog Who Could Not Be Caught

Karen Scott

Abbott Press books may be ordered through booksellers or by contacting:

Abbott Press
1663 Liberty Drive
Bloomington, IN 47403
www.abbottpress.com
Phone: 1-866-697-5310

Because of the dynamic nature of the Internet, any web addresses or links contained in this
book may have changed since publication and may no longer be valid. The views expressed
in this work are solely those of the author and do not necessarily reflect the views of
the publisher, and the publisher hereby disclaims any responsibility for them.

Any people depicted in stock imagery provided by Thinkstock are models,
and such images are being used for illustrative purposes only.
Certain stock imagery © Thinkstock.

ISBN: 978-1-4582-1293-1 (hc)
ISBN: 978-1-4582-1294-8 (sc)
ISBN: 978-1-4582-1292-4 (e)

Library of Congress Control Number: 2013921311

Printed in the United States of America.

Abbott Press rev. date: 8/26/2014

abbott press®
A DIVISION OF WRITER'S DIGEST

The story of Sweet Pea is an incredible rescue story, one that transcends the typical pet-rescue stories that people are sometimes fortunate enough to be a part of. Sweet Pea's rescue brings us to a place reached only through love and trust.

My first introduction to Sweet Pea took place one intolerably cold, early-spring afternoon in the small town of White City, Oregon, during my drive home from work. A little white, emaciated dog, with only three useful legs, hopped in front of my car on the main street leading to my home. I rolled down my window and said, "Hey, Sweet Pea, where are you going?" The name "Sweet Pea" was a term of endearment I often used, and later it became her lifelong name.

At that time, however, this dog wanted nothing to do with me or my heartfelt greeting. She scurried into a familiar hole that she knew would take her to safety. The hole dipped under a fence at the edge of a large, long lot upon which sat a dilapidated, abandoned, single-wide house trailer. The wobbly structure had broken windows and insulation hanging beneath it, but Sweet Pea was safe there.

The next day I encountered Sweet Pea again, only this time she was trapped, in a circle, by three boys on bicycles. They were hitting her with sticks and throwing rocks that they'd stored in their pockets.

I hollered at them. "Stop hurting that little doggie! How would you like it if someone did that to you?" Sweet Pea took advantage of the pause in their abuse, hopped as fast as her three legs would allow, and slipped back through her hole into the fenced lot.

The entire fenced area including around the trailer had no trees to shade Sweet Pea, and the temperature could exceed one hundred degrees in the summer months. In the winter and spring months, everything was frozen. Without trees or foliage, the ground became an ice rink. The dog's only protection was the dilapidated trailer with its insulation hanging down.

Sweet Pea foraged in the neighborhood garbage bags and cans, eating whatever her little teeth could chew. She even ate paper from hamburger wrappers and tossed-out, slimy-looking foods. Part of her foraging involved crossing a busy, four-lane highway a block away. I would follow her to the grocery store and watch her forage in the store's garbage debris.

My meetings with Sweet Pea took place daily for nearly three years. I saw her while driving to work in the mornings and on my way home in the evenings. At each encounter, I talked to her, calling her Sweet Pea.

At our home, we had two dogs and four cats, all rescues. My heart yearned for Sweet Pea to be part of the family, but Sweet Pea wanted nothing to do with humans. I observed that her abuse from the boys seemed to be a weekly thing. It is rare to see a homeless dog for such a long period of time. Usually stray dogs are killed on the road or picked up by the local animal shelter. I've picked up a few strays myself, locating their families by the collar tags or taking the animals to the shelter. Sweet Pea did not want to be caught.

I called the animal shelter. An officer called me back, informing me that the little white dog in White City "could not be caught." They had tried many times. Poor little Sweet Pea.

One year Sweet Pea had another dog friend that roamed the neighborhood with her, searching for food. They were an odd pair. Sweet Pea, with her short legs and long body, appeared to be a Corgi-Labrador mix, and her friend was a very large, shaggy brown dog. I'm not sure where the large shaggy dog slept. He surely could not fit into Sweet Pea's small hole that led into her lot. During the day, I would see them together, crossing the busy highway. Their friendship lasted about six months as they foraged for food together. Then one day, Sweet Pea was alone again.

During her homeless years, Sweet Pea may have had puppies, because I heard a great deal of barking going on inside the broken-down trailer. A year after hearing all the barking, I noticed that her belly was rubbing the ground when she ran across the road to scurry under the fence to her safe place. It looked like she was ready to have puppies. When I didn't see her for a couple of weeks, I thought she might have been run over.

On my way to dinner one evening, a friend and I saw Sweet Pea hobbling across the street in front of my car. I said to my friend, "There is that little white dog, Sweet Pea. I think she's pregnant". My friend said, "She's not pregnant. She had her puppies, eight of them." I was surprised that my friend knew that Sweet Pea had had eight puppies. We went to a nearby restaurant, but I was not able to enjoy my meal because I was thinking about Sweet Pea and her puppies.

We hurried home after dinner, and by then it was dark. I got my flashlight and binoculars and went to stand outside the fence that surrounded the old trailer. I flashed the light under the trailer, and to my absolute astonishment, Sweet Pea jumped up, barking and hopping as fast as a little white dog could. Under the trailer, eight puppy heads extended, sucking the air as though mommy's milk would be there. I was surprised that Sweet Pea was running and barking instead of staying with her pups. I found out later that "wild" dogs behave this way to distract predators from their young.

I couldn't sleep that night, as I was brainstorming how to rescue the pups and Sweet Pea. The next morning, I located the man who owned the lot. He told me that she had been around for a couple of years and had had a litter of pups once before, but he didn't know what had happened to them. He gave me the combination to the lock on the gate to his property, and I went into rescue mode.

This rescue was different from any I had ever done before, and it gave me cause for concern. How would a wild dog like Sweet Pea react to my intervention? My first step was to go inside the gate and take a look at the pups in the daylight. Sweet Pea ran off, barking again. The puppies barely had their eyes open, but they were very large for Sweet Pea to have carried inside her skinny little body.

The joyous rescue began with my calling the local Animal Shelter and Humane Society, seeking advice and asking for a humane trap. There were no available traps for her estimated size, so I called around to the pet stores, with no luck. Then I called the Havahart company, and they located a metal trap in Coos Bay, Oregon, that fit the estimated size of Sweet Pea. I ordered it.

While I waited for the trap to be shipped, I went to a friend who had the largest chain-link kennel I had ever seen, and together we constructed a safe place inside my fenced yard to protect the puppies and Sweet Pea, if I could trap her.

I stayed in communication with the local Humane Society. We made an agreement that they would help me adopt out the puppies through a local pet store where they had an adoption kiosk. Because of the intensity of this rescue, and the fact that I worked full-time, there was no time to name all eight puppies. So I just called them *puppers*.

Each day, twice a day, I pulled each puppy out from under the dilapidated trailer. I instilled in each of them some sense of self-worth, saying, "Puppers, someday, someone is going to pay fifty-five dollars for you to be part of their family. Can you believe that? Fifty-five dollars!" At that time, that was the going rate to adopt a dog.

It was mid-October. The weather was heading toward a freeze, and heavy rains were imminent. I prayed daily for strength to help this little family of dogs, as I waited for the trap to arrive. Each morning before work and every evening after work, I made up a gruel of soft foods and supplements, pulled the pups out from the trailer, and syringe-fed them food and water. Each night, I slept in a T-shirt, to get my scent on it for the puppers and Sweet Pea to get used to, then each morning, I placed it in their nest under the trailer. Sweet Pea needed no help keeping the nest area clean. She instinctively knew how to care for her young.

My first "close" encounter with Sweet Pea brought tears to my eyes. One day early on, when I was feeding the puppers, I looked under the other side of the trailer and saw Sweet Pea sitting there quietly, watching me help care for her little ones. It was a heart-warming encounter that gave me hope that she might be fine with my handling her puppers. I had been afraid that Sweet Pea, being a wild animal, might try to relocate her young to another hidden safe spot. Sweet Pea never again watched me from that spot, but she did keep the puppers where she had nested them. She even quit her efforts to distract me when I came.

Each time, after I'd finished feeding and handling the puppers, I put the pups back under the trailer and set out a bacon treat, food, and fresh water for Sweet Pea. Then I left through the locked gate. When I was several yards away, I looked through my binoculars to watch Sweet Pea as she tenderly sniffed her little ones, before hurrying to eat her bacon treat and food.

Two weeks went by while I waited for the trap. One night a heavy rain came and flooded the whole fenced lot, except for the high spot under the trailer where Sweet Pea and her puppers nested. Not knowing what to do, I became frantic. I knew the puppers would be fine coming home with me that day, but what about Sweet Pea? I did not want to separate her from the puppers and leave her alone, but more rain was predicted.

That very afternoon, the metal trap was delivered and waiting at my door. I set the trap with cat food and a small animal tranquilizer. Within minutes, Sweet Pea was trapped. I put all the puppers in a large rubber container in the back of my car, along with Sweet Pea, and took that poor, loving canine family to the safe kennel at my home.

The animal shelter had warned me to use a six-foot pole to open the trap, as wild dogs were unpredictable. However, looking at Sweet Pea, I went against the shelter's advice and opened the trap. Sweet Pea walked around the kennel, tenderly sniffing her puppers. I remained in a squatting position as I watched her love her little ones. After she was convinced that they were fine, she came up to me and rested her head on my knee, looking at me with her sunken eyes. I fell in love with her.

Sweet Pea and one pupper the morning after being trapped. Look at how huge the pupper is and Sweet Pea had eight of them.

Sweet Pea the morning after being trapped. Her right shoulder and broken leg, she is very emaciated.

The next day, while heading to the vet's office, we drove past the house trailer that Sweet Pea had called home for nearly three years. I was horrified to see that the whole area under the trailer was completely flooded.

Sweet Pea and her family all went to the vet that morning. The puppers were all very fat and healthy, as Sweet Pea had given all her nourishment to them, along with my efforts to feed them gruel twice a day for two weeks. Sweet Pea's future was uncertain, as the vet informed me that she most likely would not make it. She was near death from emaciation and looked frightful! There was also the issue of her right leg. I had her X-rayed and found out that, sometime during her homeless years, she had severely dislocated her right shoulder and had broken her leg in multiple places. Whatever had caused Sweet Pea's broken leg, she had endured it all on her own.

Puppers blessed with "cute"

The day came when the puppers were old enough to be spayed and neutered and given their first shots. It was time to part with the blessedly cute little ones. As I had pre-arranged with the Humane Society, I took a tub full of puppers to the adoption kiosk at the pet store. On the way there in the car, they all scurried out of the tub and made their way to the front of my Toyota 4runner. I told them they were more fun than a "tub full of puppers."

Upon arriving at the store, I noticed that no one from the Humane Society was there to help, so I set up an area to put the puppers in, found the paperwork needed to adopt them out, and stayed with them. The employees and customers all wanted to check out the excitement in the corner of the store, and the puppers were the main attraction.

Being able to stay with the puppers that first day turned out to be a great blessing, because I could tell the story of the pups' meager beginnings to all who would listen. Each day, any puppers that did not get adopted came home with me. The next day, I would bring the remaining pups back to the adoption kiosk. In a short time, all the puppers went to good, loving homes.

That first day, I adopted out the first pupper to a couple who were in their late seventies and eighties. Later, the director told me they didn't recommend adopting puppies to people in that age group, but I knew I had done the right thing in this case. This elderly couple, and Sweet Pea's pupper, stayed in touch with me, and we've had many visits throughout the years. We've formed a bond that is a warm relationship to this day. As it turns out, the couple outlived their dog, who lived with them for eleven and a half years.

Sweet Pea gained strength daily. Within months she was strong enough to be spayed. Watching her grow strong and trustful of me was more than I expected from this homeless "wild" dog. We seemed to have a bond that became a tool for teaching me an important lesson.

I too had come from an abusive situation, but humans don't forgive and forget as easily as Sweet Pea seemed to. Her example taught me skills for coping with the abuse and abandonment that I, as a human, could not forget. I grew to respect her instinctive skills for survival and forgiveness. It has been said that nature can be cruel, but we humans don't have to be. Sweet Pea, a wild dog living by her natural skills, taught me, a human, how not to be cruel.

One day, a couple of years after Sweet Pea joined my family, a friend noticed a lump on her. It must have appeared quickly; otherwise I would have noticed it, as I loved to rub her precious little body whenever she was near me. I immediately took her to the vet to have the lump checked, and learned that she had an aggressive cancer. She endured two major, invasive surgeries within months of each other in order to get her tissue free from cancer. I prayed that I could make up for her rough years by giving her at least as many years of quality life as the number of years she'd been on the streets.

As many years went by, Sweet Pea blossomed into a beautiful, loving, healthy dog. Her trust of me went beyond what any human words can explain. She loved and trusted all the people I introduced her to, and she never once showed the slightest sign of having been abused or homeless. She never tried to run away. Even with her dislocated shoulder and broken leg, she skipped everywhere, never once complaining. When she had enough walking, she simply stopped.

She had very few "doggie antics," such as playing ball or doing tricks, but she exuded goodness and empathy. When she heard puppies on TV, she would sit in front of the TV and make crying noises. Whenever I cried, as humans will do, she would come and love on me.

Sweet Pea was a well-traveled dog. We took many road trips together, up and down the western states. She loved going to the coast with my other dogs, Spots, a dalmatian, and Fido, a miniature poodle. The three of them were inseparable. The beach was her happy place, as she played in the low tide pools, swimming with her three short legs.

Sweet Pea had a coat that shed, and I had allergies, so she and Spots slept cuddled together on the living room floor instead of in my room. When Spots passed away at age sixteen, Sweet Pea was so heartbroken that I never again worried about my allergies. She and Fido slept on my bed and shared four close years together after Spots passed away. Sweet Pea had a wonderful snore, which I will forever miss.

Sweet Pea, Fido and Karen
at a Southern Utah Health Spa

Sweet Pea visited people in hospitals and adult foster care, sharing her love with those less fortunate than she. We went to a health spa in Palm Springs, Southern Utah and San Juan Island. She was a people-magnet everywhere we traveled, captivating people's interest as she skipped alongside me on our walks together. I think her favorite place was just being near me.

Sweet Pea on Whidbey Island, 6 months before she passed away. She doesn't look like the same dog who was trapped.

Sweet Pea lived with me for thirteen years and four months. She died peacefully in my arms, of old age and another round of cancer, but she died with all her beauty, never again looking as she had looked on the day I trapped her.

Sweet Pea's resting place along
with Spots and three cats.

Sweet Pea's life story demonstrates the miracle of what love and trust can do. I was the lucky person she chose to love and trust, as were all who were fortunate enough to meet her. She was my life teacher. I'm proud to share her story, with the hope that it will help all who read it to be kinder to animals, and to humans as well. Sweet Pea would want it that way.

Bath Time

Sweet Pea and Fido

Sweet Pea and Spots

Fido and Sweet Pea

Sweet Pea Halloween Pumpkin

Sweet Pea,
The Best
Living Thing

All Ages

Printed in the United States
by Baker & Taylor Publisher Services